SEASONS OF THE SOUL

A Faith Journey in Verse

By Joette McDonald

Seasons of the Soul
Copyright © 2013 Joette McDonald
All rights reserved.

Some of these poems have been published in periodicals, in poetry
contest publications, or may be contained in anthologies. Some have
been used as lyrics by Dr. Leslie Adams.
All poems in this volume are the property of Joette McDonald and may
be used by permission.

Cover photo by Dale Grygier

This book is dedicated to my faith family at
Grace UMC, Vermilion, Ohio and
especially to my spiritual sisters, Ladies of Grace
and my buddies in the choir.

Foreword

It would be nice if our faith were as rock-solid and immovable as God's love for us. Unfortunately, since we are human, this isn't the case. We have times of absolute unmitigated belief, and times of doubt. I was really glad (for my own selfish purposes) to read that Mother Theresa lived through dry spells, when she could not sense God's presence in her life. Made me feel better about my own struggles with faith. But, remember, Paul pointed out that our faith is an ever growing, ever changing part of our lives, and that we "press on toward perfection."

These poems were written over a period of more than fifty years, and somewhat reflect ups, downs, boring stretches and sharp corners in my own faith journey. I think there are more up poems than down ones; perhaps because I am more likely to write when I'm feeling good than when I'm in a snit or battling moments of depression.

It is my hope that you will find some line or word that describes a feeling you have dealt with, whether awe-filled worship, or a moment of doubt.

I hope some will make you laugh.....I believe God has a sense of humor....and that some will lift you up, or otherwise fit the mood you are in.

Joette McDonald
Vermilion, Ohio

CONTENTS

ADVENT POEMS

MARY'S SONGS

CHRISTMAS

EASTER

SEASONS OF THE SOUL I

There are moments of doubt,
  moments of fear
Times of unwavering, absolute faith.

There are days of pure wonder,
  And breath taking awe
 But sometimes there's anger and grief.

Thanksgiving erupts,
  In our joyful receiving,
Yet periods come when
  Contact seems gone.

Yes, living has seasons…
  Peace, pleasure or pain.
We must live through them all
  on the walk with our God.
Harvest awaits at the end.

SEASONS OF THE SOUL II

When tender buds are putting forth,
    Praise the Lord for Spring and youth.
When flowers burst to brilliant bloom,
    Praise God for joy, for zest, for truth.
When leaves are turning red and gold
    Praise Him for harvest we can reap.
When winter's winds bring frost and snow
    Praise God for rest, for warmth, for sleep.

In all our days, whatever comes,
    Our Father hears our prayers, our praise,
And we rejoice in health or pain,
    In peace, in conflict, all our days.
We choose to worship you, Oh Lord,
    When rich, when poor, when young or old.
You are the sunshine and the rain.
    You bless each season of our soul.

PSALM

Lord, I'd like to write a hymn for
you
A powerful hymn of praise and joy
Expressing faith and worship,
Evoking endless truth,
Stirring heart-felt passion.

But David used up all the good lines.

ACTS 12

The angel came and loosed the chains
and drugged the guard with sleep.
Dauntless, Peter walked away,
     his destiny to keep.
What binds us now?
What holds us fast?
What walls prevent our goal?
Our lack of courage forges chains
     ennui binds our soul.

The housemaid opening the gate
Fled from the man in shock—
Believers, unbelieving, left poor Peter
     there to knock.
Do we persist in our attempt
     To reach our ordained fate,
Or, turn away disheartened when
     The answer comes so late?

And when our angel sets us free
     And those who know us best
Are loath to open up the door,
     Can we withstand the test?

MEDITATION

How difficult it is for me
To be in fellowship with Thee!
So many blatant colored lights
flash here and there
to charm my sight.
The world intrudes and fills my thought
Distracting me from what I ought
      to be about.

I sadly find
Those shallow trifles pull my mind
away from deep and sweet communion.

My wandering thoughts
prevent our union.

I meet You when I meditate.
Lord, teach me how to concentrate!

AMAZING GRACE

I've sung it always, but failed to understand
What grace truly is—!

Unmerited and unbidden it comes.
It comes to bless
the blandest, blindest life with total joyfulness.

Now, I sit silently in awe
accepting what that sweet song means to me.

I stretch my empty hand and find it full.
I stand on move-less rock, in ever-moving sea.

How often I've accepted
unearned, priceless treasure;
Smiled, and carelessly received love,
 beyond human measure.
failing to perceive the source,
too slow to turn and face
That One who freely proffers
 amazing, boundless grace!

PETER'S MOTHER-IN-LAW

The mother of Peter's wife was ill,
in bed with a fever and pain.
The days lay heavy. She had no will
to move from her room again.
The distant sound of the city astir,
the noise of the family's chatter
were a blur and a roar to her.
She tried to shut out the clatter.

Then Peter came home with a stranger,
  a man,
He touched her. Her troubles grew dim.
Her resolve was strengthened.
  "I think I can,"
she said; then got up to serve Him.

As we lie, frightened, in spiritual dread
He can touch us, can fill us with nerve.
Let us abandon that pitiful bed
And get up determined to serve.

PAUL

That burning spirit of desire
To set the gentile world on fire
With heat of God's redeeming grace
With brand of Christ, lit Paul's keen face.
Perhaps in bonds he rode to Rome,
But freedom's truth propelled him on.
Those streets he walked echo his call:
"Come! Catch Christ's flame!"
--the Psalm of Paul

QUESTION

Is it bigger than a breadbox
 Or smaller than a tomb?
Is it brick and stained glass windows
 Does it tower? Does it loom?
Is it structure, or just people?
 An attitude, or place?
What's its mission? What's its purpose?
 Does it threaten? Does it grace?
Is it set aside for worship?
 Is it bounded in by prayer?
Do we visit it on Sunday,
 Or are we forever there?
Is it struggle or commitment?
 Does it fill a human need?
Is it covenant or promise?
 Is it built by faith or deed?
Is it Jesus, universal,
 Or the two of us alone?
Can it live in isolation?
 Does it name us as its own?

The more I think about it
 The less I think I know.
Tell me what the Phrase *"the church"* means
 And why Christ died to make it so.

FINALLY, THE POET

Christ, you were the poet, inscribing words on air;
incising verse in hearts of men,
You had no papyrus or pen,
but yearning phrases fell about you, everywhere.

Christ, you were the artist, painting portraits on the wind;
Laying color on the colorless
bright strokes within the dark abyss
expressing the expressionless,
bringing emptiness to end.

Christ, you were the sculptor;
carving monuments of time;
finding form in ancient laws,
chipping out the subtle flaws.
erecting clean, pure angles, and unrelenting lines.

Christ, you were the poet;
Your words the whelming flood,
each line an arrow in my soul
each verse clearly written by your blood.

THE POWER TO HEAL

There's so much pain and hurt today,
Oh, God, would I cause more?
I blunder as I seek to help,
My ministries are poor.

You trusted me with treasures—
Gave keys to that most dear--
Have I betrayed your confidence?
Are my intentions clear?

There's so much pain and hurt today.
Here at the cross I kneel.
Please lead me, guide me on the way
You have the power to heal.

YEARS AND SNOW

Here it is, Lord, the year you chose to give---
It lies before me like the clean snow
       outside my window.
Shall I lie down,
       trustingly,
           face turned skyward,
              and make snow angels?
Shall I build a fortress, Lord,
       or an arsenal of ammunition
           for protection?
Shall I build a castle with turrets
       and tunnels
           and a banner on top,
Or should all my efforts
           be directed toward
              building snowmen?

Perhaps I'll shovel, hurriedly,
       seeking to clear the way
           hoping to discover what's beneath.

Help me, Lord.
       I can't delay or dally
           over decisions.
Years and snow
       Don't last long.

YEAR OF JUBILEE

All is forgiven, my debts are erased.
The ground I had lost
    Is completely replaced.
I heard the rams' horn
    And exultantly knew
The time of spare poverty's
    Finally through.
Jubilant, jubilant,
    Rise to the year.
The age of redemption is here!
    Is here!

Cast away credit cards,
    Mortgages burn.
Cancel out interest.
    Reap the return.
He paid the piper!
    Don't beggar the fee!
Dance on the promise!
    Jubilee! Jubilee!

TIME TO SOAR

While waiting for the Lord
  Mount up on eagle's wings—
Climb above annoyances,
  Recognize the strength.
Exult in boundless energy—
  Accept the limitless
Explore the new frontiers,
  Breadth and length.

O, Lord, I'm soaring now!
  I feel the lift of love.
It's dizzying and dazzling,
  And great.
I wish I'd learned much sooner
  The absolute rewards
That come to those who learn
  To trust and wait!

PROVERBS 8

Can't you hear the voice of wisdom
Crying from the city gates:
"Listen, You, stop being foolish,
Seek the Lord while he still waits.

Wisdom's wealth is more than rubies,
Knowledge brings unending worth.
Listen, You: Seek understanding.
Know the Lord, and own the earth!

OUR FATHER'S HOUSE

This is your house, Father.
Here we can feel at home,
     loved, safe, cherished.
Whatever we do to embellish
     This dwelling place
Must also embellish You.
        Any window installed must open.
Any door put in must never
     Close anyone out.
An ambiance of love
     Is not merely desired,
        But necessary.
Designs must lift us upward,
     Glorify you,
        Yet,
     Gratify us inwardly.

Our Lord was a simple man,
     Creating warmth.

Can His house be otherwise?

PARADOX

He will conquer you bless you,
Bring you down to elevate.
Stop you suddenly to move you,
Give you haste to make you wait.

Lord of gentle paradoxes
Let me bow to your command.
I surrender! I surrender!
White flag waving, cede my stand.
Make me lose that I may win.
Plant my feet on solid ground

ANSWERED PRAYER

I shouldn't be surprised, Lord,
My amazement convicts me.
You said you'd hear and answer---
And, yet, I doubt.
Then, when proof is offered,
Stunning evidence of your direct work,
I'm bowled over,
Breathless,
Wide eyed!

I'm chastened by my unbelief,
But joyous, Lord,
Overwhelmed
By your response!

PARABLE

I've spent my life searching
In cracks, in the dust
For the coin I am missing.
Lamp lit and glowing,
I grope in cobwebbed corners
And shake out muddy mats.
All my inheritance,
Shiny and precious
Is heaped on the table,
A tribute to life!
But one piece is missing
And I'm disconsolate,
Unfulfilled, incomplete.

What joy when I find it!
I'll celebrate wholeness
And shout it to you
When seeking is over and
Goals are completed,
The angels in heaven rejoice!

ECCLESIASTES 11

The time has come
> when bread cast carelessly,
>> lovingly
>>> upon the water
>> returns.

> I kneel joyously
>> on the shore
>>> and gather it
>> in glad astonishment;
Basketsful of crumbs
> now turned to amber.
Gemstones
> with just the shadow
>> of the deed within---
Now multiplied
> miraculously magnified,
>> and beautiful.

>> Beautiful!

SOMETHING NEW

"I will show you a new thing,"
    God said,
And there was Christ—
    Always fresh
        and compellingly simple.
Always surprising,
    not weighed down
        with old baggage.

A new thing;
    and there was a soul
        purified,
    washed and refined,
        the past winnowed
          by cleansing winds.
    the stale, rotten layers
        of ancient sins
        peeled away.

And underneath,
    behold!
God shows us a new thing.

SERMON

If you never leave the nest, he said,
Your soul will surely starve.
Security can be stagnation,
And risk is part of living.

As eaglets must be pushed to fly,
You, too, must leave and dare
To trust that it's God's
Loving nature to be giving.

(based on a sermon by Rev. David Palmer, 1987)

TALENTS

I didn't bury it, Lord,
   but I'm not clever
      at making investments.
The market's unstable!
  Is it poor stewardship
      to gain no returns?
What if I lose the principal, Lord--?
     Will I be censured more
        than if I'd hidden it
         safe?
    Or, do you give credit
      for risk taking?

PRAYER

Lift me up from
        mires of doubt.
Turn my skeptic spirit out.
Lead me where the paths
        are clear
let me leave my blundering
        here.
Fill me, Lord,
        With simple trust.
Scourge and try me,
        if you must.
Christ, I long
        Your face to see.
Bring me closer, Lord,
        to Thee.

GRATITUDE

Thank you, God!
I say it a thousand times each day
Knowing that it's not enough,
No matter what I say.
For all you graciously supply
I never could repay.

But, Father, I'm so grateful!
I rejoice as you bestow—
Accepting, gladly, gladly!
And praising, as I go.
Why You should choose to bless me thus
Is more than I can know.

I know I'm undeserving
And selfishly too proud—
Why should I reap happiness
When tears engulf the crowd?
In this, my glad acceptance,
My heart is humbly bowed.

Thank you, God and Father—
Bless others mercifully.
May those in loss and anguish
find solace, is my plea.
May other recognize the joy
of being close to Thee!

A TEACHER'S PRAYER

God, help me, just for tomorrow
To have a patient heart
That hears the underlying pain
Some children always bear—

Help me to understand the needs
Within one student's life,
And guide my lips
To say that thing that eases hurt,
To fill that need that looms.

Tomorrow, Lord,
Put healing in my hands
And lead me in my dealing with each one.
Give me the power to lift,
And not put down.
Teach me the wisest way to reach a mind,
To fill a heart.

Let every little one within my care
See your eyes shine through my striving,
And feel that nurturing love
Beyond what I, alone,
Can give.

NEWS FOR GOD'S CHILDREN

Children, children, gather near,
Embrace the news I bring!
Put aside despair and fear—
The golden age I sing!
It's time for peace and unity.
His promise leads us on.
Find joy! Take heart! Expect the best.
Emmanuel has come!

Do only children see it?
Do only children hear?
The message hasn't changed, at all.
The song is still as clear.

Become a child! Accept the joy!
Believe the truth I bring.
Pause in your ceaseless journeying,
To hear the angels sing.

THE BINDING

You, Lord, are cover to my book.
Without you, my pages flutter,
    Scattered by the wind,
        Lacking narrative or pattern,
    Chapterless and unresolved,
        Plodding, plain, and dull.

You bind and collate randomness,
    Build in a rigid spine;
        Collect and give direction.

Editor and publisher
    Of my raw manuscript—
    Affix your copyright
        Here, here, here
    On my soul.

ROMANS 8:28

"All things work together"---so Paul said—
    And I believe him—
"For the good of those who love the Lord."

Sometimes the work
    is strenuous.
Sometimes the "things"
    are painful.
Sometimes we fail to notice
    tiny movements toward the good.

But, we must believe the promise,
    and so, endure the waiting,
for the work that brings us closer
    to that "good" that
translates: "God."

If we love Him and we wait,
    our time will surely come,
We shall receive the good.

REAL ESTATE

We take the concept of your universal love
And create narrow, selfish strips.
We build fences of exclusion
And guard them with our lives,
Despising those who dwell
Outside our self-defined enclosure.

Father, we divide the sweep of your concern,
Determined none shall share,
If the shape of their homesteading
Does not align with ours.

Lord, we stake a claim,
Declare that holding OURS!
We clutch tightly in our small domain
That grand, eternal truth—
We are all your heirs, we are all your own—

But—The inheritance is OURS!
We deny those in another room
The coin of your redemption,
And make bristling subdivisions
Across the landscape of your love.

CONCLUSION

I believe I've reached the promised land—
Believe I've crossed the river,
Dwell in days of milk and honey,
Securely in your hand.

The fields are filled with fatted calves
The vines bear fragrant fruit.
Living water bubbles forth.
The desert has gone green.
You've straightened every crooked road.
You've made defilement clean.

Lord, thank you for each day!
--each hour--
      of dwelling in this place.
And thank you, thank you, Father,
For your unremitting grace!

THE ROAD
(a hymn)

(Chorus)
You never promised us it would be easy.
A mindless path was never what you planned.
Yet, we can hear you say
You'll be with us all the way
If we will reach and take you by the hand.

The road is not a curve-less course of pavement.
Sometimes we make a turn and go astray.
We often reach a place
Where crossroads interface
Forgetting you will guide us, if we pray.
(*Chorus*)
There are detours, and we long for four lane
                          highways.
There are looming hills and treacherous terrain.
Some chasms gape and yawn
The tiring track runs on—
We're winded, and we start to feel the pain.
(*Chorus*)
Someday we'll reach the point of destination.
We'll understand how roadblocks made us strong.
No more weariness or grief,
We'll find joy beyond belief
At journey's end, with you, where we belong.

SABBATH

You're the sunshine in my garden.
You're the Springtime in my soul.
You're the rainfall that refreshes.
You're the rest that makes me whole.
And I believe
And I receive
And I welcome blessed Sabbath
That draws me close to You.

In the busy-ness of living
I forget to draw apart
To accept the glad renewal
You've prepared to fill my heart.
Help me believe
Help me receive
Help me just be still and listen,
Take the time to be with You.

When droughts have scorched my gladness,
When clouds have dimmed my view,
Help me pause and just remember—
I need time alone with you.
Let me believe.
Let me receive.
Let me go apart and seek you
And find strength and joy anew.

ABOVE ALL ELSE

Above all else, you lift me up,
And ever, near the light
I walk on pathways paved with gold
In gardens of delight.

I have no right, I pay no fee
Yet, you hold out your hand,
And, smiling, lead with certainty
Toward that promised land.

What perfect joy to know your touch.
Beyond my reckoning
The calm assurance in my soul
That you alone can bring.

Dear God, I have not words nor time
nor method to repay—
Thanksgiving bubbles in my heart
And colors every day.

THE NEED

Lord, are you silent,
　　or are my ears too dull to hear
　　　　and fully understand?
Lord, are you absent
　　or are my eyes too blind to see,
　　　　too dazzled to discern
　　　　　　the shape of crown or hand?

Lord, are you near me?
　　Or is my perception flawed by the profusion
　　　　of finite, earthly, useless things?
I need re-sensitizing:
　　A lesson in awareness,
　　　The selfless, open spirit
　　　　That pure communion brings.

PLOWING THROUGH THE O.T.

We followed Moses through the wilderness,
Raised our eyebrows at the sinning—
God and Moses had a row to hoe
With those tribes, from the beginning.

Perhaps we failed to feel their pain,
To understand frustration.
We never truly empathized
With the wandering Jewish nation.

If ours had been those hot, dry tents,
If we ate manna, daily
We, too, might see the darker side,
Not sing God's praises gaily.

We yawned through passages of law,
We chaffed to hurry through it.
Exodus, Leviticus—
Just set your teeth and do it!

COMMITMENT

Yes, Master, I'll feed them—
If only I can.
I carry my basket, thrust out,
In my hand.

Their bleak eyes are lifted
Their nostrils expand
To test if I offer them chaff
Or real bran.

If you'll only fill me,
I know that I can.

WOMAN AT THE WELL

Beside the well the world looks dry and barren.
I pause and wipe my sleeve across my face.
The weight of empty jars
      are as the world upon my back.
I come alone, at midday, to this place.

Beyond me lies the desert, hot and endless.
Behind me lies a town that knows me well.
Within me stirs despondency and absolute disgust ,
For I have made my life a private Hell.

And then—
      The stranger speaks to me! He greets me!
He offers perfect cleansing and release.
When I retrace my pathway, my heart brimming,
as my jars,
I've traded in my turmoil for His peace.

PROBLEM

Grace cannot be bought or sold.
It's a gift, so I've been told.
Open up your heart, they say.
God's love will fill it, right away.

I desire it, but there's a catch…
My heart has a faulty latch.

THE BLIND MAN

You're passing by!
I hear the clatter of the crowd.
I feel the dust that rises from their feet.
I've waited here since dawn.
I knew you'd surely come—
Now, pause, and make my broken life
       complete.

You've got to stop and listen!
You've got to turn and smile!
You must be moved to pity
       by my cries.
Nothing in the world
Will ever be the same again…
If you'll only lay your hand
       upon my eyes.

PLEA

The milling crowd about your feet
    has made it hard to see.
I'll occupy so little space,
    please, save a place for me.
My hesitation isn't doubt.
    I'm certain of my need.
My poverty incriminates.
    I'm loathe to bare my greed.
But, Lord, you promised room for all,
    No matter where or when.
I take one step, though tentative.
    I know you'll take me in.

THIRST

My spirit is so parched and dry,
I've stumbled from the stream.
I'm crazed with thirst,
  the void inside has overcome my dream.

I wildly seek to find a way
To the waters of belonging.
Come, o holy spirit, come,
And satisfy my longing.

CHRIST AT A WEDDING

Christ at a wedding,
 a visit divine
Laughed with His friends
 and turned water to wine.
Out with the old!
In with the new!
Christ celebrating,
and miracles, too.

Take thou my life, Lord,
tepid and bland.
Touch my earthen vessel
with your powerful hand.
Cleanse me and change me;
the brackish refine.
Add color and flavor
and turn me to wine.

WHO IS GOD?

You, our God-almighty—
      Exalted and supreme—
You hold the universe
      And eternity in Your hand!

Yet—Sometimes we assign to You
        The role of Santa Claus.
    We post our North Pole prayers
      In child-like expectation.

Sometimes we reduce You
      To the role of our employer.
      We work for You! You owe us!
      Our prayers are applications
      For the salary we're due.

Sometimes we relegate You
      To a distant, frozen mountain.
      We cast our prayers like grains of sand
        carried by the wind,
    expecting no response.
    nor acknowledging, when it comes.

continued→

(continued)

Sometimes You seem to us
        The local emergency squad.
        We forget You, 'til we need You,
        And then, we screech for help.

Sometimes—oh, yes, the list goes on!
        Yet, Lord, we know you're none of these—
        although all of them, and more.....

So high as the heavens are above the earth
        Are You, past understanding,

Thank you, Father, thank you!
        There are not words nor space
        Nor time
        In our brief, mortal span
        To adequately express
        Just who and what You are.

JOHN WESLEY'S WISH

John Wesley said
"Don't let me outlive
 my usefulness."
And I concur.
May I occupy this space
only so long
as what I do can benefit
some other.

Our days are filled with joy
when there are
opportunities
to serve You, Lord.

AT CHURCH

Whatever else You gave us,
     Love's the catalyst we require
To make adhesion lasting,
     To comfort our desires.
We've formed a tiny, precious knot
     Along the strand of time;
A compacting of separates.
     A meeting of the minds

It must be You intended this.
     I see it on each face.
We've just become Christ's body
     For one moment,
        in this place.

INTERPRETATION

Lord, send a sign to me, today,
    That I may do your will.
Then send a good decoder
    Well-engineered, and real.
So often I've encountered
    Your charming hieroglyphs.
I'm fascinated, totally,
    But fail to catch their drift.

CHOICES

We know that Hell is any moment
      Spent apart from You.
Yet,
        Willfully, we choose the darkness,
          Spurn the proffered light.
We've failed to weigh and measure options,
      Our judgment's all askew.
That sense of knowing
        What is best
Has not developed, quite.

So, we choose Hell,
      And suffer.
So we choose Hell,
      And cry—
You seek to make contact with us,
      Each day!

      The stakes are high.

THE FULL ARMOR

Excuse me, Lord.
I know I'm not wearing
Just the proper attire.
Righteousness, Paul said,
Is an armor,
Protecting and projecting
An image of faith.
My shield is slightly rusty
And the breastplate's loose
And insecure.
The helmet doesn't quite
Cover all it should.

I hope you'll overlook
The dents and dings and nicks.
I know I ought to shine!
But I thought, perhaps, maybe,
It's the coat of arms that counts!
And there it is, Lord,
Emblazoned on my shield,
Bold as day—
Your name!
Will you let me in your army?

BURYING DOUBTS

Lord, help me dig a grave in sands of doubt
  and there bury
      the cynic,
      the skeptic.
      the wry questioner
  who've lived with me for years.

Lord, help me fill that hole
    with hope and trust,
    plant deep the seed of faith,
    water it with your word,
        and fertilize it well with prayer.
    Help that shoot sprout upward
          to shelter
  every bird of joy and peace you loose.

  Make me a witness tree
      for You,
          oh, God.

THE MIDNIGHT OF MY SOUL

In the midnight of my soul
  You are the candle
In the winters of my heart
  You are the flame.
In the maze of weary days
  You're the compass and the chart
When I have lost my way,
  You call my name.
When every step is labor,
  You're the wayside inn.
When every thought brings pain
  You soothe and calm.
In time of deep despair
  I know You're always there,
Of numbered reassurance
  You're the sum.
When joy is like a sunrise
  You're my smiling friend.
When life is filled with choices,
  You're my guide.
When love is mine to share
  And hope is everywhere
You're the peace that knows
  No limit, deep within.

(set to music by Dr. H. Leslie Adams)

MANNA

Lord, deliver me
    from the trap I build,
        baited with my own comfort.
Save me from savoring
    my own small triumphs
        and open my awareness
toward others' needs.

Yes, the manna you provide
    is satisfying.
Help me to discern
    the desert beyond,
        that I may gather
            basketfuls here
in my own private Eden
    to distribute
        in the wilderness
            in your name.

RECOGNITION

"Look over there," she cried,
      Pointing to where
It glimmered with the clarity
         of a star.
    "What is that?"
"Why, it's your neighbor's soul,"
      He answered.
"But, my neighbor was so—
        ordinary.
    So unremarkable!
I never dreamed he'd
        shine like that."

"Every man," He said,
    "Contains eternity
        At the center."

THE SEARCH

Who is this man?
      Who is this Christ?
I seem to brush near him at every turn.
Others tell me they know him well.
They say he causes their hearts to burn.
I feel his shadow across my life
And reach to grasp what's almost there--
They tell me it's fire,
      And I sense the warmth.
But something further I need to learn:
Some way of looking that I've ignored.
Some way of framing the proper prayer
That will start the flame
      To bring the glow
And cause the light for which I yearn.

GIVE ME SERENITY

I ask, Lord,
        For a quality of serenity
That will calm and reassure
        These fragile minds.
Let me be a stable, secure
                place
Where little ones can
                come
to feel safe and soothed.

Help me remember
        it's easier to think
In an atmosphere
            of trust
        and peacefulness.

Let me be a haven
        For your children, Lord.

PETER WASN'T PERFECT

Peter wasn't perfect,
John was fraught with faults,
Thomas had his moments of despair.
Each man had his vanity,
And felt sharp pangs of jealousy:
Knew times when understanding wasn't there.

These men, the closest to you
Often seemed they scarcely knew you.
They stumbled as they struggled,
    but they grew.
Thank God for all their blemishes!
Thank God you said you loved them,
For, with all my warts and weaknesses
I know you love me, too.

ADVENT POEMS

HOPE

When problems loom and grief appears
Hope whispers gently in the ear—
"Look up! Take heart! Don't feel oppressed,
Be confident, withstand the test!
For Christ has come to conquer fear!"

When days are dark and laughter dies
Hope comes to make the spirits rise.
"Hang in there! Fight! You're bound to win!
Keep trying! Pray and don't give in.
Christ comes. The heavy burden flees.

When doors are closed and light is gone
Hope lends a hand and leads us on.
The windows open. Sun streams through,
Christ comes and all things are made new.

Hope on. The promises are true.

PEACE

The angels sang a hymn of peace
    In Bethlehem, long years ago.
And from that Savior, manger born,
    Came forth the sweetest peace we know;
Peace of spirit, peace of mind.
Peace that touches all mankind.

O, loving Jesus, feel our need
And come with healing touch, we pray.
Pour heaven's gifts throughout the world.
Let conflict cease. Bring peace today.

    Peace of spirit.
    Peace of mind.
Peace that blesses all mankind.

JOY

Like a bubbling fountain
    Rising in my soul
Joy so rich and beautiful
    Fills, and makes me whole.
Surging through my moments,
    Washing grief away.
Mighty flood of purest joy
    Brightens every day.

Why this sound of laughter?
    Why this urge to sing?
Sadness and despair are gone.
    For Christ is Lord and King!
Sadness and despair have flown,
    Our blessed Christ is King!

LOVE

More powerful, more gripping than forces of death,
More tender and gentle than a new baby's breath,
Universal, pervasive, as broad as the sky
Focused and small, it points out you and I

Stirring, yet healing, it calms and excites.
It satisfies longing, it pains and delights.

O, Precious Redeemer, you taught us God's plan
To love you completely, and our fellow man.
How warming, how lifting, how beautifully plain:
The love you gave to us we must give back, again.
The seeds of that love, which you plant in our soul
Transforms and enriches us, making us whole.

This, then is Christmas, the message so true;
Because you first loved us, we must love you.

(can be sung to the tune of Immortal, Invisible)

SONG FOR THE CHRIST CANDLE

As the seed of salvation and promise, you came
Bringing hope to the needy who call on your name.

At the jagged outer limits of our bleakest grief you stand,
Compassion written in your eyes, hope held in your hand.
When pounded by confusion, or strife that does not cease,
You come, with gentle, calming words to bring us perfect peace.
There , at the dark abyss of guilt, the brink of our despair,
You raise us up on wings of joy, you banish every care.

O, wondrous child of Bethlehem,
        We offer songs of praise,
We're filled with humble gratitude
        For the love, that brings us grace.

ADVENT

Prepare a manger in your heart
Upon this Christmas Day.
Spread swaddling clothes upon the straw,
And clear the chaff away.
Then, filled with joy and wonder,
Go spread the word this morn:
"Have you not heard? Within our hearts
The infant Christ is born!"

PEACE

Here at the center
A circle of peace.
Lamplight and starlight
The limits define.
Terror and conflict
And hatred must cease.
Brotherhood, amity,
And good will entwine.

Christ is here!
Christ is here!
Sing it again.
Endlessly, gloriously,
God's love will reign.

MARY'S SONGS

MARY, DO YOU REMEMBER?

Mary, do you remember
The lights above the hills?
Mary, do you remember
The night the stars stood still?

Mary, do you recall
The hush of wonder, the mystery
Mary, help me remember
How soft and how tender
     His love comes to me.

Mary, do you remember,
Do you remember
How shepherds knelt in awe?
Mary, do you remember,
Do you remember
The angel hosts you saw?

Mary, do you recall
The light of heaven on his face?
Mary, help us remember
We must surrender
Our wills, to win his grace.

LULLABY

Sleep my little one
Lie still upon my breast.
I know the world is waiting,
But stay, and take your rest.

Tonight you light my life
With tender, infant smile.
Stay close within my arms, now,
You're mine but for a while,

Soon tomorrow comes, child.
Life calls out to you.
All the earth is waiting
With things that you must do.

Now, sleep, my little one.
Lie still upon my breast.
I know the world is waiting;
But stay with me, and rest.

(set to music by Dr. Leslie Adams)

MARY"S SONG I

How long ago it was when I awoke that night
To the radiance of His presence in my room.
I still recall the wonder,
How it made my heart stand still;
The awe that I was chosen—
That the seed of man's salvation
The holy one of Israel was implanted in my womb.

The years have plodded onward
Like camels on the sand,
Floors to sweep and meals to serve,
And clothes to wash and mend—
And the baby, grown to boyhood,
With scratches on his knees,
With the alphabet and laws to learn,
Games among wood shavings,
And classes at the synagogue a man-child must attend.

He grew, as children must, he learned, as children do.
But there was something more,
Kept and pondered in my heart.
The fires of joy that smolder,
Banked with ashes of the future,
The radiance! Oh, the radiance, still remembered
Is my part.

MARY'S SONG II

Little boy, my precious little one
　　　With eyes too wise
And tender love imprinted
　　　in your infant smile.
Stay in my arms.
　　　Let me hold you and rock you,
Stay. Be my own little one for a while.

The clamor of time,
　　　The call of the waiting world
Bids you to hurry and grow.
Tomorrow you'll fulfill your destiny's role—
Tomorrow you'll answer the urgent demands—
But, stay,

Let me sing you to sleep again, Child.
　　　Stay.
Be my own darling son
　　　For a while.

MARY'S SONG III

There was word this week.
John said he saw him
near the sea where boats are made.
He's taken up with fishermen,
Not kinsmen of our family.
He spends his time in teaching,
Doesn't follow Joseph's trade.
John said the crowd was angry.
Did they hurt him? Is he hungry?
John said his face was weary.
Does he have a place to sleep?
I had hoped he'd choose Rebecca
And settle near the marketplace,
Or somewhere here in Nazareth;
The old traditions keep.
Yet, inside I know—I've always known
His calling doesn't lie along familiar ways.
John saw him, though. He said his touch
    holds healing,
His words echo like thunder,
That the love my boy is teaching
Lights a candle, these dark days.
There was word this week.
John says that he is well
And about his father's business.
There was nothing more to tell.

MARY'S SONG IV

The glory of the sunrise!
      It warms and comforts weary bones.
My step is slow
      And faces move as shadows
Yet, the brightness and the lightness
      And the glory flood my soul.

When I was young the promise came,
      And filled me with delight..
My body now, has borne the crush of time
      Yet, the promise still stands strong.
I'll lay aside this worn-out shell
      And move into the light.
He waits for me and beckons,
      And I'll move into the light.

CHRISTMAS

THE STAR

For an instant the star shone again
     And hearts looking upward could see
The secret of starshine that always has been,
     The truth of eternity.

And the magic of love captured thus in a soul
     Glows on, undiminished by years.
That star that shone just for a moment apart
     Becomes constant, and outshines our fears.

CHRISTMAS QUESTION

Where were we that Christmas night?
Were we scrubbing or cooking
      Or herding our sheep?
Celebrating with friends?
Putting children to sleep?

Were we too harried to hark to the star?
Too busy with commerce
      To notice the choir?
Distracted by living
      Did we miss the light?
Where were we, that Christmas night?

Where are we, this Christmas Day?
Will we stop by the manger one moment,
      To pray?
Can we slow our frantic, harried routine
And pause by the stable to worship the king?
For one instant will shopping and
      Gift wrapping cease
While we find at the center
      The Prince of Peace?

Where are we, this Christmas Season?
In our gay celebration, is Jesus the reason?

GENTLE CHRISTMAS

How soft across the writhing world
The cloak of peace is flung.
How gentle in the pounding din
A tender bell is rung.
For eyes unwilling to perceive
No star can ever shine,
Nor, will the tightly compressed mouth
Taste sweetness of the wine.

He comes to us with silent shout
To bring god's powerful word.
Those attuned to voiceless hope
Will smile, when they have heard.

THE LION AND THE LAMB

O, Little Lamb,
     Don't fear the lion!
See, he comes in peace.
Lie quiet as he crouches near
     And bid your tremors cease.
The promise is for sweet accord,
     For days unmarked by strife.
The child is born.
     he brings his love
To ease the storms of life.

A LITTLE GRIL'S SONG

Tell me, Pretty Lady,
What's your baby's name?
May I come inside the stable
And have a little peek?
I do believe it is a boy.
I like him, just the same.
May I put out a finger
And touch his tiny cheek?
I'll be so very gentle.
I know that he's asleep.
I won't make any noise.
He'll never know I came.
Tell me, Pretty Lady,
What's your precious baby's name?

SONG OF THE INN KEEPER'S CHILDREN

O, Sister, look yonder,
      out there in the night—
O, why is that star
      a'shining so bright?
The mules are all stamping,
      the cows in their stall
are mooing and moving—
      what's causing it all?

O, sister, just listen!
      What's that that I hear?
It sounds like a church choir
      So pretty and clear.
I thought I heard voices—
      A lady was hurtin'.
But now it's so peaceful and quiet,
      I'm not certain.

O, sister, there's something
      out there in the shed
come on and wake up, now!
      Let's get out of bed.
How can you be so sleepy and slow?
There's something, there's something
      Worth seeing, I know.
(set to music by Dr. H. Leslie Adams)

HAPPY BIRTHDAY, BABY JESUS

Happy birthday, Baby Jesus.
Here we kneel before you,
Lay aside our cares and pride
To perfectly adore you,
Singing happy, happy birthday, Little King

All the turmoil of this world
For this one moment ceases
While we wait with open hearts
To learn of you what peace is.
Singing happy, happy birthday to the king.

May the truth of brotherhood
That you can to teach us
Burst anew in tired souls—
Let your vision reach us,
Bringing happy, happy birthday to our king.

(set to music by Dr. H. Leslie Adams)

CHRISTMAS ANGELS

Flocks of angels settle earthward,
Ring the bedroom where I lie.
Faces all reflect compassion,
Wings a-flutter fill the sky.
Some wear draperies of remembrance
Other seasons, other years.
Some wear mist-refracted auras,
Light diffused by unshed tears.
Some bear tokens to remind me
Where my prayers should congregate.
Others swing a smoking censor,
Spread good will and dispel hate.

Angel legions come to comfort;
Offer healing, conquer gloom,
Gather, singing soft hosannas.
Christmas angels fill my room.

THE HANGING CHURCH IN CAIRO

Joseph took his wife to Egypt;
His wife, and infant son.
The magi had informed him
That he'd be wise to run.
Did they travel on a donkey?
Did they camp along the way?
Were they ferried to the other shore?
Was it their plan to stay?

There is a grotto near the Nile
And, whispered down the years,
Are stories of the holy child
And of his tenure here.

God called His son from Egypt.
"Come home. , Re-cross the sea.
Herod is dead. Come home, now.
Come back to Galilee."

PRAYER FOR THE NEW YEAR

We ask not, Lord, for blessings heaped
On those we have today,
Or for a year better than the last.
Give us, instead, eyes to see that what we have
Will be that "happy yesterday" when it is past.

Teach us to use these things we know and own
With pride, and love,
Since they are gifts from thee;
Not wasting any precious slice of time
But relishing each crumb
From that great loaf, eternity.

We ask not for a year that brings a brighter day;
The sunshine of your love is still the same.
We only have to turn to face the blinding ray
To know the happiness our hearts may claim.

Bless not the year, Lord, but the day.
Keep us alert, keep us awake, keep us aware,
That every fleeting joy a day can bring
Is butter on our slice of time.
          And you are there.

SOLITUDE

If I sit still and silent
    And turn off conscious thought,
If hands are folded in my lap,
    And bright distractions
        Tucked away,
If I open empty bins of mind,
    And purge them, as I ought;
Seal off selfish introspection—
    And then, just sit and wait—
Will my spirit flutter upward
    Like a grey, excited bird?
Will God's hand reach to capture it
    And feed it with His word?

SHH!

I stormed your gates
    With tempest,
        And with flailing.
My wailing rose
    To smite your
        Fine tuned ear.

You answer came,
    As soft as
        Dandelion down.
And, I, amidst my raving
    Failed to hear.

THE GIFT

It often seems,
Dear Lord to be
The gift that you have
Given me
(Ironically such treasure
You extend.)
Is bigger than the "me"
I keep it in.

INSTALLATION

Maybe I need to install
    A spiritual computer.
I've made a royal mess
    Of things.
        And could use
    Some wise programming.

I need some button
    I can push,
Some floppy disc
        With bytes and bits
To interface my mind with yours
    And print it out, complete.

O, Lord,
    Send an expert
From some celestial IBM
    To help me
        Organize my soul.

A MEETING OF FRIENDS

Homespun pulled around his shoulders,
firelight on his face,
Cooking fish upon the seashore
at the end of day.
"Love's the word,"
He tried to tell them,
"Love and deep concern."
Echoes skip across the water
as the campfire burns.

How they longed to keep the moment!
Inexplicably, it passed.
Waves erased campsite and footprints.
Only love can last.

WOMAN IN THE CROWD

The dark, fetid oozing that will not stop,
But ever wells from secret recesses
Draining the essence,
The vitality,
The quivering cytoplasm from the cell of self
Is unstaunched.
It's the wearying continuity,
The losing of self
In an endless flow
That tears at the mind.

Somewhere in this crowd
There is a garment
With dust fringed edges
The moves just above the filth-strewn street—
If I can only reach it—
Find rough fibers with my fingers,
Contact the hemline,
It will be enough.
The sudden, electrical jolt
As the power circuits through me
Will cauterize and cleanse me,
Seal the welling source of infirmity,
Will heal—
If I can but touch
The hem of His garment.

CHANGES

Lord, when I found out who you were
I fully changed my mind.
I changed my style of living,
Changed what my goal's about.
I changed priorities and hopes.
Yet, daily, Lord, I find
I've changed a lot of things for you
But failed to change my mouth.

CHURCHES OF MY YOUTH

Every Sunday was Good Friday
    In the churches of my youth.
Word like hand-shaped iron nails
    Hammered piercing points of truth.
Blackened crepe draped every altar,
    Every sermon bore a cross,
Lifting up a gentle Jesus
    On our throes of guilt and loss.
Stark and real the hill of Calvary,
    Hard as straight-backed wooden pews.
Unadorned, no stained glass windows
    Filtered stern, judgmental views.

Yet,
    The friend we have in Jesus
    Eased the burden of our sin.
Love and reason rose, triumphant.
    Joy was victor, in the end.

THE MIRACLE

The miracle is
    that you cast out
        the demon, fear,
And let an angel of confidence
    flutter in,
        on satin plumed wings
to fill up the space.

The miracle is
    that believing in you
        I can believe in me—
Trusting you,
    we can
        trust ourselves!

You teach us self love
    that we may love others.
And that's the truth.
    That's the miracle!

GOD OF NEW BEGINNINGS

Oh, God of new beginnings,
    Help me finalize an end.
When a phase, at last, is over,
    Help me face it, not pretend.

Oh, God of things eternal,
    Help me learn to love the hour---
Grasp that only you are lasting,
    Trust In your enduring power.

Oh, God of all the ages,
    Help me bury now, the past.
Lead me up to new tomorrows,
    Free to do your will, at last.

SAMPSON

Sampson lost his hair,
    Then blind and heavy hearted
Recognized at last—
    That Yaweh had departed.

I grapple with my head.
    The hair is there, in place…
But, can I see with certainty
    The blest redeemer's face?

Sampson knew his strength
    Had roots that lie in binding vows.
Lord, have I shaved off my pledge
    And lost contact, somehow?

ISAIAH

Reveal your face in majesty
Too blinding for my eyes to see
I'll peer through fingers, tense with awe.
My being seared by what I saw.
And if the thunder as you speak
Leaves mind and maverick body weak,
Perhaps when I recall the glow
And hear the echo, strength will grow.

Against my stained lips, place the coal
To cauterize my cankered soul.
Then, I'll arise, refreshed and sure
With words of truth, and accents, pure.

SAMUEL I

Old Eli pulled his blanket close,
    And stared into the darkness.
There it was again--
    That still, small voice—
    "Here am I."
Voices hadn't touched the night
with shattering fingers for eons.
    Should he ignore it?
Perhaps he was dreaming---
    But, no.
There it was, again—
The patter of small, bare, feet.
    the childish voice.
    "Here am I."
Why, Eli thought,
    Why is that child calling out.
    Interrupting sleep,
    Making a rough place in time,
Changing the pattern,
    Spelling disinheritance?
"I haven't called you, child,"
    Eli answered,
"It's the Lord. The Lord called.
    Answer him."
In the darkness, he heard the voice
    of obedience,
The voice in the night that sealed his fate.

BILDAD

A friend of Job,
    I sit at a distance
        from the dunghill,
upwind, and near
        a bed of daisies.
Not close enough to see or smell
    the draining corruption
        from the boils.

There, sheltered by distance
        from the odor and pain
I urge him to take heart,
        take heart!
The sun will shine tomorrow.
    God will smile,
        heal hurts,
    dry up oozing sores,
        restore wealth.

Upwind,
    I can be smug and wise.

JACOB

It's so easy, you say,
    To let go and let God.
But I can't do that.
    I'm always wrestling,
        hip out of joint,
    across the river.
Somehow I never comprehend
    the dawn,
Never loosen my hold
    to receive
        the blessing.
Blindly, like an automaton
    programmed to grapple
        I seize and struggle
    only taking time
        for a peaceful breath
between rounds.

IMPERFECT FAITH

Imperfect faith, imperfect love
I give to you, imperfectly.
And, in return, you give me grace,
Peace and joy, eternally.
A heart, half-hearted, I extend,
Thoughts divided, prayers half-prayed.
But Your acceptance is complete
Of each piecemeal petition made.

Inversely doubled love You give,
Exponentially increased
Such algebra I cannot live,
Nor grasp such theorems, in the least.

Though undeserving in my need,
I clutch your bounty, filled with greed.
Yet,
You linger, waiting, still,
Lest I perceive your perfect will.

DENIAL

Peter, Peter, weep for me,
    For I've denied Him, too.
The cocks are crowing everywhere,
    Pale dawn is breaking through.
Not only thrice, but thrice times thrice
    I've shoved the truth aside.
Please, Peter, plead my case for me.
    I've no place left to hide.

ACCCEPTING TOUCH

Oh, thank you, Lord, for being
All wise and ever kind;
For keeping all Your children's needs
Eternally in mind.
At times our cries are foolish,
Self centered and absurd.
Yet, gently, you still answer all
Who call upon your word.

Oh, thank you, Lord, for patience
When we demand too much,
for healing our unworthiness
With Your accepting touch.

When we face grief and losses
From making such poor choices
You hear our urgent voices.
For this, we thank you, Lord.

THE CIRCUIT RIDER

Christ rode in triumph to Jerusalem!
In honor of this
You, with due humility slogged over
miry, marshy trails,
Rode through mountain passes
bent against solitude
and hunger.
Pushing back fatigue or fever;
Arriving alongside pioneers—
Sowing seeds of salvation
on newly claimed land,
clearing away brambles,
pushing on to new frontiers
of faith.
No palm leaves strewn before you,
but your own joyful satisfaction
on the endless circuit
of homesteading for a humble savior,
against all odds.

LET THERE BE SILENCE

Lord, for one moment,
      Let there be silence.
Hush the roar of engines
         and machinery.
      the insistent pulse of music,
the ever-present syrup and clatter
         of background tunes,
        Shush those clamorous ,vapid shows
         with in-your-face ads
that crowd the airwaves
      and press us incessantly.
Quiet the shrill, demanding
      land lines ,
         the inescapable grip
          of our implanted
        cell phones and iPods.
Quell the sonic boom
        of getting here to there
           too fast.

Bring silence, Lord,
      for one crystal moment.
And then,
      Into that precious silence:
        Speak.
      And we will hear.
        your still, small voice.

AWARENESS

When I am made aware
Of who you really are—
When I can grasp but faintly
The scope of what you mean,
Then I'm in awe to find
That you consider me,
Creator and redeemer,
Eternal deity

My selfish supplications
Are inward turned, and small.
My words lack depth and substance
Even as they leave my heart.
The wonder is that You
Turn ear to me at all—
The marvel is, you hear me,
Almighty as you art.

I love you, God and Father,
With flawed, imperfect love.
I praise you,
But my words are trite and shallow.
Teach me how to fashion
Prayers worthy of your praise.
Help me find the words and voice
Your holy name to hallow.

SAIL ON

We've seen some stormy seas,
    some knotted lines,
Some moments when recaulking
    was required.
We've had some days when
    we just lay becalmed;
Felt the journey was not all
    that we'd desired.

But. a wiser hand was at the wheel
    to guide us,
To teach us how to come about,
    to tack.
He helped us ever realign
    our heading
so there would be a fair wind
    at our back.
The voyage, now, is mostly
    joyful sailing,
with sunlight and a gentle,
    steady breeze.
How blessed we've been to
    have a skipper
Who guides us,
    when we fall upon our knees.

DISTRACTED PRAYER

Lord, I'm not much good at prayer,
Though I'm addicted to it.
I start out one direction—
Then never do get through it.
The world intrudes and scatters thought,
My concentration's poor.
Your magnet heart compels my mind,
And doesn't close the door.

I ask for more than I deserve,
Lift those I love to you,
Then feel a pang of guilt that I
Am selfish, through and through.

You made me, so you understand
Those places where I fall.
That's why the words I use in prayer
Are "thank You!" most of all.

RAINBOW'S END

I've spent all my life
    Out chasing shadows,
Out seeking treasures, or friends,
Fooled by glitz and glam
    That don't really matter.
Yet fully knowing You're
    The rainbow's end.
It's easy to be fooled by
    Wanton promises,
Easy to be tempted by desire.
Easy to become a doubting Thomas
Even when I feel my heart on fire.

I've walked through all the deserts
    And the jungles,
Trudged down trails
    That caused my heart to bleed,
I made many foolish choices,
    Many bungles
Before I learned it's only you I need.
Looking back, I see that little's lasting.
We grasp at things that move or twist or bend.
But, your eternal truths are ours,
    For asking:
The pot of gold
    That marks the rainbow's end.

PRAYER FOR RETICENCE

I talk too much! Oh, Lord, I pray
Teach me to monitor the things I say.
Help me to curb the impulse to attack
Some unsuspecting one behind his back.
Teach me to turn off at a touch,
And not appear to think I know too much.
In every sentence help me reach my goal
And never carelessly put down another soul.

So often peace of mind
     Upon a word is hung.
Lord, my sin's
      Mostly centered
        In my tongue.

DIETER'S PRAYER

I eat too much. Oh, Lord I pray
Help me to curb my appetite today.
Help me to be content with "just a touch"
And know instinctively when I've had too much.
My body is your temple, Lord, it's true.
Teach me to keep it well, for You.

Help me love fish and lettuce more than sweets.
Keep busy fingers occupied—but not with eats!
Make chocolate abhorrent to my taste,
And   roast beef less important than my waist.
A fat-free body should be manna to my soul.
Teach me control,
       teach me control,
            teach me control.

(partner poem to "Reticence")

MENDING

Oh,. God of bits and pieces,
    You understand our stress.
Collect the fragments of our lives
    And heal our brokenness.
We scatter energy abroad,
    Uncertain of our goal.
With your unshaking, careful hand
    Collect and make us whole.

Untangle frenzied, hopeless knots
    Smooth over conflicts, please.
Restore some order in our world.
    Make of our pieces peace.

MARK 4

You taught them, Master,
           as you walked.
They listened, passing near the sea.
Scant time for sitting rapt in thought.
They learned while traveling with Thee.

The best things they would ever know
Were lessons, spoken on the way.
Not pausing in your traveling
You spoke with wisdom, every day.

So, mingled with the dust and sweat
           and set to rhythmic foot-fall's beat,
The journey they were on with you
Used head and heart as well as feet.

It hasn't changed. We move along,
And you instruct us, this we know.
On life's short trek
           we walk with You;
Listening, learning, as we go.

UNANSWERED PRAYER

It didn't work out the way
       I wanted it to.
It didn't turn out the way I'd planned.
I turned it over to you, Lord.
      Did you not hear?
      Did you say no?
Is there something I still fail to
       understand?

It seems so wrong this way.
      Did you just shrug it off?
      Is this my punishment?

It didn't come out
      the way I'd made petition for.
Was my pleading all in vain?
Something else I should have done?

Oh, Lord, my God, have you forsaken me?

      Why, Lord, Why?
      Why? Why? Why?

EASTER

GOOD FRIDAY

We push the replay button
And the seasons cycle back—
The momentary glory,
The triumph of His entering—
The sudden, bleak betrayal,
The evening stark and black,
The frenzied mass of people,
Christ painfully re-centering.

We read the timeless message
And struggle to perceive
the shock of distant hammer strokes
Exploding in our head.........

Help us increase our faith;
The agony relieve.
Don't let us wander, aimlessly,
        in disbelief, instead.

GOOD FRIDAY, OLD HURTS

Take them out, today,
    and nail them on that cross,
      lifted high.
Nail them with your bare brain,
    battering
      blunt pointed memories,
Impaling anger and despair
      there
    midway up the air.
Search them out,
    parade them through
      your conscious lanes
lined with jeering, shouting
    shards of ego,
      ready to shame and blame:
Old misguided stabs at truth.
Lash them, if you will,
    with strands of twined reproof.
Then, lift them, bleeding, up,
    Up on the cross of forgiveness.

And, as the pain subsides,
    at last,
      forgive yourself.

Even as He forgives.

THE MOTHER

"I once had a child like you," she said,
      Her mother-face crumpled with grief and strain,
      As she tenderly touched the baby's head,
And in memory touched her own man-child again.

"He was laughing and bright, a loving lad,
      Much more than a son and a child to me.
His years near my side made me glad, yes, glad!
Though I knew in my heart
      What the end must be."

She caressed this young stranger, then turned away
      To look with sad eyes across distant hills.
      "I loved him so, as I do today—
Ah, would I could shelter and comfort him still."

She walked slowly apart, for her task was done.
      "It's his mother," they whispered,
      And moved aside,
To watch as she wept for her son, her son!
Then left him alone on the cross
      Where he died.

DAYBIRTH

I lift my train across my arm
And run toward the sun.
My footsteps in the dew-wet grass
Are all I leave behind.
And yet
And yet
Where blades are bent
Perhaps some following feet may find
The certain joy that comes
When all if heaven's dome is lit
By this glad surety:
I am a child of God
I am a child of God
I **AM** a child of God
I am a **CHILD** of God
I am a child of **GOD**!

Too large a concept to contain
Within the hollow of my hand;
I throw it to the wind
And laugh.
At last, at last, I understand:
I—Am—a—Child—of—God.

(set to music by Dr. H. Leslie Adams)

PAINTING FROM STORY'S CHAPEL

Jesus walked upon the water,
Held out his hand and bade us come—
This compelling invitation
Is enough excuse for some.
The water flowing from his eyes
Those fountains of the Giver
Cascade across my firmament,
Unite, become a river.

That stream propels us onward yet,
No looking back, no sighs.
I'll walk upon the water, then,
And straight into the skies.

GRADUATION

Goodbye, my friends,
My teacher said my tenure here
is near an end.
The principal's in place to convey the honors of
matriculation.
What a joyful schooling it has been--
Although the tests were difficult
and sometimes painful.
--But, lessons, classmates, school--
Such a pleasant, fulfilling journey!
--And the teacher!
Oh, the teacher was sublime!
So wise, so caring and so understanding:
Always there to help, instruct or guide.

So, now I'll exit happily
knowing that ahead
is eternal, marvelous, boundless learning.
A graduate school with only honors,
and never, ever the pressures of exams!
I accept my diploma with joy.
Goodbye, my friends.
I'll meet you on that beautiful, celestial campus---
Yonder.

TODAY'S REQUEST

Father, here is another day.
It's dawned so clear and so blue
That I ask as I rise to meet it;
"What can I do for You?"

You've done more for me than I can recount,
(Much more, I am sure, than I know!)
If we are taking things turn about
I'm badly in debt.
   And so,
If You'll just point out some little thing
A one-talent person might do
I'll sleep tonight
With the knowledge bright:
I did what I could for You.

LAITY LITANY

What can I give, poor as I am?
Three apple pies and a picnic ham
Last year's clothes for the rummage rack
And a box of useless bric-a-brac
For the auction sponsored by circle four
Chocolate chip cookies for the baked goods store.

What can I give? No problem here.
There's a dozen benefits every year
To raise the funds so the church can live
Without the tithes we are meant to give.

THE SIN

The sin is not in losing
We are told, but in not using.

The organ may not be in tune,
The fingers not be sure—
But, go on, play it, anyhow;
And if the chords aren't pure
At least the rust won't grow,
The fingers won't go stiff.
What if the talent's small?
God promised us that if
We don't use what we have,
He'll take that, too, away.
So, sit down at you organ
And play, and play, and play!

QUESTION

How can God be big enough
    To twirl that farthest star,
To plan those unknown planets
    My childish soul may ask.
The breadth and scope of galaxies
    Expanding is too far
How can God be big enough
    To tackle such a task?

I stretch my narrow mind as wide
    As narrow minds will go
Still, I can't understand how God
    So infinite can be.
Yet, big He is! My soul, expand!
    Behold infinity!
Yet small....so very small
    That he can still
        Consider me.

SPRING SONG

God said "love" and it was Spring;
Gently, gently, it was Spring—
Golden green and lavender
Touching every living thing.
Flinging hazy, lacy nets
Up the hillside, down the bank
Golden-green and softly pink,
Rows of trillium, rank on rank.

God said "Spring" and it was love,
Tender, sturdy, tingling,
Golden green and violet;
God said "love" and God said "Spring."

BLESSING

How blessed, how blessed, how blessed I am
By you, of, King of Kings!
Your bounty overwhelms my soul—
Your gifts outweigh my fondest goal.
I'm left with only words of praise
And with a soul that sings.
Your gifts are wrapped in human touch:
Companionship and smiles of friends,
In glad encounters, without end.
Oh, Lord, you've given me so much!

Yes, we are your children,
We're sisters and brothers.
We see you most clearly
In the faces of others.

WORSHIP

Worship transcends worldly trappings
Outlasts our contrivances.
Souls can soar above the tangle,
    Reaching for eternal truth.
Great creator, strip the wrappings,
Pierce the armor of defenses
See within us aching, longing,
    Cores of seeking for our God.

Worship overcomes excuses,
Looms much larger than our reach.
Recognizing power and greatness
    Soothes and comforts,
      Brings us peace.

JUST FOR TODAY

Lord, help me squirrel away
      Enough of laughing and of listening
         To last me through the day.
Lord, help me dump self-pity
      In the early afternoon
And incinerate my selfishness
        Before the rise of moon.
Lord, guide my thoughts
      On gilded wing
And give me joyful,
        Outward-visioned songs to sing.

If the world I'm in is so narrow
      That it holds but me, alone,
Please father, bring the sundown,
        And quickly take me home.

DISCIPLES

I know you spoke to Moses
    In the thunder and the fire,
You spoke to trembling shepherds
    With majestic angel choir.
You called to youthful Samuel;
    He answered "Here am I."
And you stopped Saul's persecution,
    Struck him down and made him blind.
Your voice is of the moment.
    Your messages are clear.
Choose the manner and the moment.
    Let us hear! Oh, let us hear!

FOCUS

When bad things happen
And we're focused on chaos and evil
We forget to be grateful
For all of the good.
Thank you, Father,
For families that are functional,
For children
Who are bright, smiling and directed,
For communities where people
Reach out to one another
For the interwoven fabric
Of love and care and friendship
That binds us together
As one people;
Your people.
Thank you
For schools where teachers strive to teach
For healthy, positive activities
That build our minds and bodies
And for the beauty and
Absolute mystery of your creation—
This world, in which we live.
Thank you, Lord!

CONTRIBUTION

Melt what gold I have
        And make
      a vessel to be used in time of worship.
Gather any gifts I own
      to be used for You alone.
Anything you've given me
        I will return.
        I will return.
Gather any gift I own
      To be used for You, alone.

Pour the balm that forms my spirit
      on the sorrows of your children.
Anything you've given me,
      Gather in!
      Gather in!

The bounty in which I revel
      You have loaned me for a day.
I must quickly pay it back, again,
      Before it fades away.

SONG

Pipe me the tune again,
> Shepherd, tonight.
Light me the star again,
> Guide me aright.
Sing me the song again,
> Fill me with awe.
Show me the child again,
> There on the straw.

Pipe me the tune again
> Joyous and clear.
Trembling with promise
> And sweet to my ear.
Filled with pure wonder
> Eternally new.
I'll hear it, and kneel there
> To worship him, too.

ENCOUNTERING CHANGE

My longing soul cries out, O God,
in days of wild uncertainty.
When all that's grounded disappears
and moves must be made cautiously.
When slipp'ry hands must scrabble hard
at swiftly moving, teflon time—
No finger hold, no place to stand,
the road ahead a rugged climb.
Stability is what I seek
in quagmires of seductive change.
My soul cries out:
 Please, help me find
one solid place, one view not strange.

The door is there.
        I must but knock
to find a haven firm and sure,
a foothold on the changeless rock,
to rest in you; complete, secure.

THE PARABLE OF THE TALENTS

Since I could not be like Mother Teresa
    And feed the hungry thousands,
I did not make my neighbor's lunch.
Since I could not sing like Callas
    And thrill the waiting world
I refused to join the choir.
Since I could not be like Michelangelo
    And paint the Sistine Chapel
I would not draw the cover
      For the Sunday School program.

My talents are too small.
It's embarrassing to reveal
    Their flimsy meagerness
    To the world.

Then Christ said:
    "You were the salt of the earth,
    But you clung to the safety
    Of the shaker
And the world has not been seasoned.

?

What if…..
  I came to God
    For help
And He said
    "Take a number."?

13th CHAPTER of 1st CORINTHIANS
(tune: Chariots of Fire)

Though I speak with tongues of angels and men
If I have not love, my words are in vain.
Though I know the future, can mountains remove,
My power and knowledge are nothing, to love.

  Love's patient and kind
  It does not boast,
  Love never is rude.
  Love doesn't count wrongs
  Or flaunt itself,
  It's honest and good.

  Love never is proud or envious
  Love always can cope,
  Love's trusting and fair
  It thinks the best.
  Love always has hope.

When wise words are silenced
  and prophesies fail
When knowledge has vanished,
  still love will prevail

Though I speak with tongues of angels and men,
if I have not love, my words are in vain.

LETTER TO AN ANGEL

Hey listen up, Girl!
You've lolled about too long,
Collecting feathers, painting rainbows,
Learning caterpillars songs.
I've been around and looking—
Poking and probing everywhere.
No matter how I perservate
And wait. And wait.
You're never there.

Hey, pay attention, Girl!
Accept your bounden duty.
You've got a full-time job with me
Providing love and beauty.
You may be bored and tired of me.
Perhaps you yawn.
Or curse your luck.
But come on, Guardian,
Be on guard!
You may not choose me,
But you're stuck!

FUTURE OCCUPATION

If I can choose then I would opt to be a guide—
That voice, serene, assuring
At the end of the dark tunnel;
The hand that holds the light,
That reaches, comforting,
To steady shaken souls.
The smile that reassures.
If eternity stretches endlessly before me,
Then give me employment,
The warm glow that only comes
From helping others.
Lord, if I can petition you,
If I prove worthy of regard,
Then give me a place on the border,
One foot in the nether world.
Perhaps it's hubris, Lord, to ask to be
A guardian angel—
It's not the wings and halo
That I covet, but the job.
What bliss to escort doubtful,
Shivering spirits
Into celestial light!
What blest reward to lead others
To *their* blest reward!
I beg of you, Lord, let me be an active member
Of your work force, when I move on.

PARADE IN ST. MARTIN

When Jesus came to Front Street
      He wore a shirt of red
And all the laughing children danced along.
The drums pronounced their cadence,
      A trumpet fanfare led
the band of stalwart marchers in their song.

Standing up for Jesus
      the Christian soldiers came
Past fast food and casinos
      tee shirt and jewelry stores
And did the watchers know Him?
      Maybe. Maybe some.
Some chose to join in,
      others to ignore.

When Jesus came to Front Street
      the traffic stopped for Him.
Mothers rushed their sons
      to join in the parade.
Blue skies reverberated,
      the noise of commerce dimmed,
And blisters, from the drumming,
      was the sacrifice some made.

134

ARE YOU THERE?

I long to see your face.
      Oh, show me you are there.
I need to hear your voice.
            Just tell me you are there.
Please, let me feel your touch.
            Assure me you are there.

I feel my empty prayers
            Bouncing off the ceiling.
Have you rejected them,
                  And me....
            Or, are you really there?

RENEWAL

The rain comes,
   Sweet,
      Refreshing
         Penetrating;
      Awakening
My parched, dry soul.

I open to welcome it,
      Renewed,
         Ready
      For the following sunshine.

Always, always,
      Your blessed love
         Brings me back
      To full flower.

JARIUS

"Too late, Oh, Christ, my child is dead!"
The frantic, grieving Jarius said.
"I called, I knew she couldn't last,
And now the time of healing's past."

Come, Christ, the situation's dire!
We need your cleansing, healing fire!
The need is vital! It can't wait!
Don't tarry, or you'll be too late.

How soon, how soon we all forget!
We know how Jarius' plea was met.
How weeping parents soon rejoiced--
For the child arose at Jesus' voice!

Impatiently our prayers are said.
We grieve, our shattered hopes, now dead,
Too late, we think, to ease our strife
or wake new meaning in our life.

Come, Jarius, tell your tale anew,
That we may accept Christ's miracles, too.

Hmmm?

"God chasteneth whom he loveth"
So the scriptures say.
I feel so warm and cherished---
Has God then, turned away?

PROBING DEPTHS

What depths to probe,
　　　What heights to rise
What vistas fill my doubtful eyes.
To open windows,
　　　Calm the storm
Feel the current
　　　Embrace the warmth.
The daily boring,
　　　plodding pace
The thin events cause minds to race.
To curb the impulse,
　　　Still the chaos
Inhale the beauty,
　　　Seek the cross
O, Christ, be with me
　　　While I find
What calms the storm,
　　　What stills the mind.

LISTEN
(*meant to be sung*)

(chorus)

> *Listen, listen!*
> *The lord might be a-talkin' atcha!*
> *Listen, listen! Just be still!*

Speech and music and noise
Hammer through our days
Phones ring, iPods sing,
Symphonic sounds amaze!

(chorus)

News and politics,
Bold, warning words abound,
Traffic roars, confusion soars
There's clamor all around.

(chorus)

Turmoil can rise and insist
Without an interlude
The world crowds in with vice and sin
Committees press and intrude.

(chorus)

God, still our racing minds
And soothe our frantic days.
Help us be still
And do your will.
Please teach us, Lord, to pray!

(chorus)

THE NEED FOR TEARS

Oh, God, if I could only cry!
Please, give me tears
    To cleanse , erase, renew,
A stream to mellow dull, encrusted
      Corners

Oh, Father, please let me cry!
    I need to cry,
Elixir , balm for the soul.

Each tear might be a searing torch
    Burning away hard surfaces,
Each drop a sandstone rasp
    Smoothing rigid, petrified resolve,
Each streak along the cheek
    A lane toward a gentler time,
    A softer understanding,
Each episode a thunder storm
    Washing away the doubt and
      Barren emotion,

Oh, God, just let me cry.

ECCLESIASTES 2

Vanity! Vanity! All is vanity—
    Oh, preacher from that bygone time,
The truth of what you said to us
    In your poems lingers on.
Enjoy your work! Seize the day!
    Don't dwell on what may follow.
No matter how you measure things,
    They're bound to turn out hollow.
Praise God, trust and thank him,
    whatever you may find.
No sense fretting over it;
    You'll never know His mind!

Vanity, vanity! All is vanity!

THANKS

At this stage
Only two words
Remain:

Thank you.
Thank you.

Thank you!

READING THE GOSPEL OF MARK

Hie yourself hither, and hastily so.

Mark says "immediately,"
    So, come on. Let's go!
Time's of the essence.
    That's perfectly clear.
Christ saved mankind
    In only three years!
Three years of teaching,
    Outlining His plan.

He acted immediately!
    The rest's up to man.

ROMANS 8:36

How wonderful it is to know
    That nothing separates us;
No power on earth, great or small
    Can keep us from Your love--
Or keep your love from us.

No hulking threat,
    Real or imagined
Deters your gentle, reassuring touch.

What promise!
    What hope!
What absolute relief
    It is to understand
The eternal, changeless gift
    That's given us.

Oh, Father, pry my fingers loose.
    Open that tight fist I've made.
Help me, at last to grasp the truth:
    You're here.
    You sent your son.
It's all we'll ever need.

FLOW, JORDAN

Flow, Jordan, flow.
        Not a foaming stretch of water,
But a narrow, gentle stream,
        Lovingly embraced by green
Like a sweet, refreshing dream.

Your waters still revive us,
        Cleanse us, make us glow.
There we can be washed and purified.
        Flow, Jordan, flow.

VARIATIONS

God's always, always the same—
    So we're told.
We can rely upon that
    --and on Him.
But me—
    It depends on the hour
Or the day or the week we are in,
    On the year ,
    On my mood
        Or the state of the world.
You never quite know.
    I just go with the flow.

Thank you, Father,
    For staying the same.

About the Author

Joette McDonald has been writing poetry since she could first pick up a pencil! She has had the pleasure of teaching fourth graders creative writing skills and sharing with them her love of the classics. Many of the poems contained in this volume were originally written as the verses for her handmade Christmas cards. The home she shares with her husband Joe is   filled with the love of their children, grandchildren, great-grandchildren, exchange students from three continents and friends from many corners of the world.

For more information contact:
Joette McDonald
4005 State Road
Vermilion, Ohio 44089
joejoette@roadrunner.com